The Strength of the Hills

A Portrait of a Family Farm

BY **Nancy** Price Graff

PHOTOGRAPHS BY **Richard** Howard

Little, Brown and Company

BOSTON · TORONTO · LONDON

We would like to thank the people who helped make this book possible: William Jaspersohn, for invaluable advice; Michelle Gumpert, for research; Bill Paine, for directing us to the Nelsons; Bob Harnish, for the quiet to write; Harriet Price, Helen Benedict, and Chester Liebs, for reading the manuscript; Maria Muller, for printing the photographs; Linda Paradee, for technical advice. Special thanks to the Nelson family — Bill, Jenny, Grant, Hannah, Andrew, Betsey, Howard, Evelyn, James, Fremont, and Marsha — for opening their barns, houses, and lives to us so generously. To Jenny, especially, we are deeply indebted.

Library of Congress Cataloging-in-Publication Data

Graff, Nancy Price, 1953–
    The strength of the hills : a portrait of a family farm / by Nancy
Price Graff; photographs by Richard Howard.
        p.   cm.
    Summary: Portrays life on a small family farm in Vermont by
describing a single day in the hard-working but prideful existence
of its owners.
    ISBN 0-316-32277-6
    1. Family farms — Vermont — Juvenile literature.   2. Farm life —
Vermont — Juvenile literature.   [1. Farm life — Vermont.]
I. Howard, Richard (Richard Huntington), ill.   II. Title.
HD1476.U6V547   1989
338.1'3'09743 — dc20   89–7950
                                                  CIP
                                                  AC

10 9 8 7 6 5 4 3 2 1

Published simultaneously in Canada
by Little, Brown & Company (Canada) Limited
Printed in the United States of America

To my children, Garrett and Lindsay,
and my husband, Christopher
N.P.G.

Also, to farm families everywhere
for nourishing us in ways without measure
with the fruits of their labor
N.P.G. and R.H.

In the summer

in Vermont, the days unroll like green ribbons, long and seamless. By four-thirty in the morning, the rising sun has already begun to melt the blankets of fog that settle during the night among the hills and along the rivers. Seventeen hours later, the sun draws the last of its light over the mountains and hills to the west. In between, the sun arches hot and high over acres of meadow and pasture and forest.

This is a time for growing. Out in the fields the corn grows an inch a day. Hay is mowed and begins growing back even before the tractor is returned to the barn. In the golden warmth of the sun, alfalfa, sweet timothy, and other grasses with names as soft as summer itself tangle and thicken into vast green carpets that run like roads over the land. Everywhere beneath the soil, new roots are spreading and reaching, creating and feeding life.

But the roots that go deepest on the Nelson farm in Ryegate Corner are the roots of the Nelson family. They go back one hundred and seventy years on this same land. Only the stone walls that line the fields are older. They go back nearly two hundred years, to a time when the earliest settlers moved to this corner of northeastern Vermont and began clearing the land. But as far as anyone in Ryegate Corner is concerned, Nelsons have always lived here, farmed this land, milked the cows that crop these pastures, and kept this

house painted white, this barn painted red. This is the story of life on the Nelson farm, where Bill and Jenny Nelson live with their children, Grant, Hannah, Andrew, and Betsey, and of the kinds of work it takes to tend and hold on to one small corner of the Earth, generation after generation.

The rising sun is Bill Nelson's alarm clock twice a year, once in late March and again in late September. On those two mornings, Bill and the sun both get out of bed at the same time. Every other morning of the year, the eighty-five cows waiting for their first milking tell him when to rise and start his day. In winter, it is still as dark as the heart of night at five-thirty when he gets up. In summer, the day is already an hour old.

Bill eats the first of his two breakfasts alone in a house still quiet and sleepy. He eats light, a cup of coffee and a doughnut or piece of pie left from last night's supper, while he spends half an hour reading magazines and newspapers covering farm news from around the country and the world. At six, he puts on his hat and walks out the door, across the yard, the road, and the barnyard into the milking parlor to start milking. It is the way every one of his family's days has started for seven generations.

Modern equipment allows Bill to milk more cows than his father or grandfather or great-grandfather could, but it also means that milking is no longer as simple as sitting down on a stool beside a cow and milking into a bucket. The Nelsons' milking parlor is really two rooms, one with twelve stalls for the milking cows and another with a fifteen-hundred-gallon tank where the milk is collected, stored, and refrigerated until it can be picked up and taken to the dairy. For half an hour, Bill gets the equipment ready. He puts a filter in the milking system to catch any stray bits of sawdust or dirt that might get into the milk. Then he flushes the pipeline through which the milk will flow with hot water and chlorine to kill any germs that might make the milk unsafe

to drink. He hoses down the floor where the cows will stand and cleans the teat cups that will be attached to the cows' udders during milking. Finally, he sets out several buckets of hot iodine water that will be used to wash the teats before each cow is milked.

By the time Bill is ready to begin milking, his help has arrived. Paul Pearl is the Nelsons' hired man. He works six days a week, twelve hours a day, on the Nelson farm, eats his meals at the Nelsons' table, and teases the children

like a good-natured uncle. Bill's other help is his father, Howard Nelson, from whom he bought the farm seven years ago. Bill's father and mother live one hundred yards up the road. For nearly fifty years, Howard Nelson has been milking cows morning and evening. Although he no longer owns this farm, his habit of getting up early in the morning to milk is cut as deeply as a canyon through his life. Also, he knows that Bill would not be able to milk the cows waiting patiently in the barn beyond the milking parlor if he and Paul did not help.

Cows are big animals. They move through the back doors six at a time into stalls lining the milking parlor, like a freight train pulling into the station. They bump into each other and push their way to separate feeding troughs where grain is pouring down from chutes on the walls. While the cows bury their noses in their breakfasts, Paul, Bill, or his father wash their teats, "strip" or pump them once by hand to get the milk flowing, and attach the teat cups.

Once these tasks are done, it takes less than five minutes to milk a cow. The milking machine pulses like a beating heart, sucking the milk from each cow into a tube and then spraying the light golden foam into a receiving jar. When the milk is flowing smoothly, it fills the jar at a rate of one pound every ten seconds, six pounds per minute. When the udders are empty, Bill or Paul or Howard removes the teat cups and dips each teat into a cup of iodine to keep the nipple clean. When all six cows in one row of stalls have been milked, one of the men pulls a rope handle that opens a door at the front of the parlor. The six fed and milked cows amble out through this door into the barn, while Bill stands guard letting six hungry and unmilked cows push through the back doors to take their places in the stalls.

Howard Nelson remembers when he milked by hand, fifteen cows each milking. The milk went from buckets into tall, plain metal milking cans that sat in ice water until a farm truck came and picked them up. Next the milk went into vats that were emptied into railroad cars that took the milk to dairies near the cities.

The milk truck that arrives early this morning, as it does every two days, holds 54,000 pounds of raw milk, the equivalent of 627 of the milk cans that Howard Nelson once used. This is the eighteenth and last stop on the trucker's milk route before he heads to Idlenot Dairy in Springfield, Vermont, seventy-five miles away. It is the trucker's job as milk hauler to take a sample of the Nelsons' milk for testing later at the dairy, to check the temperature inside the Nelsons' bulk tank to make sure the milk has been kept cold enough to stop the growth of germs, and, finally, to record how many pounds of milk he takes so that the Nelsons can be paid for the milk their cows produce.

17

When thirteen-year-old Grant joins his father and grandfather in the milk-ing parlor a little after seven, as he does nearly every morning, the narrow pit between the cows where the milkers work grows crowded with moving elbows and rubber work boots. The morning milking is in full swing now, and the parlor hums with the energy of big animals, throbbing equipment, and men at work. Grant is as comfortable here as he is in his own bedroom. Like his father and grandfather, he could milk with his eyes closed, but like his father and grandfather, he knows better than to try.

It is difficult to talk here, but Grant is too excited not to add his chatter to the hum. His favorite cow, a lovely holstein named Judy, calved early this morning. If the calf is a worthy heifer, she will be Grant's to show next year, just as Judy was Grant's show heifer last year and the year before. Already he and his father and Paul have been out into the barn to size up the sleepy little bundle of legs and ears.

The business and hardships of farming have always been softened by mornings like this one. Judy's calf will not be spared from the work of producing milk and calves for this farm when she is grown, nor will she escape the slaughterhouse at the end of her usefulness to this farm, but the joy and hope that surround a special calf's birth are two of the reasons Grant wants to continue farming.

Such is the rhythm of production on a dairy farm that all the cows are never lactating, or producing milk, at the same time. Tomorrow morning Judy will rejoin the herd of milkers that she left six weeks ago when her calving date grew near. During that month and a half, her milk dried up and she gained strength for calving. Giving birth has started her milk production again. For several days her milk will be saved and given by bottle to her calf because it

contains antibodies that help the calf fight illness. But within a day Judy will be out in the pasture again, taking her two turns a day at the milking machines. The calf will be in a pen with other new calves, learning to drink milk from a bucket. Two months from now Judy will be "bred back," or bred again, and nine months from then she will have another calf, after first drying off again. This pattern of breeding, drying off, and giving birth is repeated each year among the one hundred and thirty cows on the Nelson farm, and keeps milk production high.

When Grant is finished in the milking parlor, he joins Hannah, Andrew, and Betsey in the heifer barn across the road for morning chores. Here are heifers too old to be bottle-fed but too young to be bred or milked. On the middle floor are calves from six weeks old to nearly a year old. They are kept tied in narrow stalls so they don't suck on each other. Once this urge to suck passes, at about a year old, the calves are moved to the lower floor and barnyard where they are free to wander. Only when a heifer is bred, close to her second birthday, is she finally ready to join the herd and move across the road to the milking barn and pasture.

Inside the hundred-year-old barn the light is soft and thin. The smell is ripe, like the sweet smell of freshly cut grass after a rainstorm mixed with the smell of old wood and fresh manure. Sounds disappear in the rustle of swallows' wings high in the rafters. Every movement of air brings hay down from the mow in a gentle drizzle.

At the far end of the barn, eleven-year-old Hannah is up in the loft pitching a bale of rowen to the floor. Last fall it took her entire family to bring in the bales of this tender second cutting of hay and load them into the loft to winter the calves in the stalls below. Getting the hay down is easier — it comes down one bale at a time, and gravity helps — but like

much of the work on the farm it calls upon arts that farm families pass down among themselves. Moving an unwieldy fifty-pound bale of hay is just such a hand-me-down art. Hannah flips it end over end down the length of the barn with the skill and grace of a circus performer.

Andrew, Betsey, Hannah, and Grant take care of the heifers and yearlings in this barn twice a day. At the moment there are fifteen calves upstairs and twenty-five yearlings downstairs. Last winter there were nearly fifty calves upstairs, and the work of carrying grain, hay, and water to them kept all four children busy for more than an hour every afternoon after school. During the school year, their mother, Jenny, takes the morning feeding and watering chores. When summer comes, she doesn't need to remind the children that the calves are once again their charges. The hungry bellowing every morning beneath their bedroom windows is all the reminder anybody needs.

Andrew is nine and Betsey is only seven, but they have been helping out with these chores since they were old enough to walk and carrying a full share of the work since each turned five. They pry open the trapdoor in the floor behind the heifers' tie-ups and shovel manure until the floor is clean. Then they spread fresh sawdust for bedding. Hannah walks down the line of heifers giving out grain, and their heads bob before her in a friendly wave. The calves' long tongues curl and stretch, trying to get extra licks from the scoop. Betsey lugs water in buckets for them, and Andrew pitches hay under their noses for them to nibble at later.

Like Grant, Betsey is happy in the barn with the music of lowing calves and buzzing flies. Even when she stops to talk or think, she automatically reaches out to scratch and rub the calves around her. She has been to a city once, but this is the life she imagines even when she dreams.

Working in the heifer barn each day, Betsey scouts for a show calf for next year. Last year Hannah was the only girl in her club to show a calf at the Caledonia County 4-H cattle show. This year Betsey knows of several girls who will be showing calves. Next year she wants to be among them. She knows she needs to pick a calf that won't have grown any higher than her chest because a bigger heifer would be too difficult for her to handle in front

of the judges. She knows, too, that she needs to find a calf that shows good signs of "dairiness." Dairiness means long, straight, strong legs; a square, solid body; a straight back; and a good size for the heifer's age. It's the language of farming that Betsey has heard spoken around her since she was a baby. Her grandfather pays her a high compliment by calling her a "good little farmer," and what he means is that she works hard and listens well.

Meanwhile, Grant has driven the tractor over with a bucketload of silage, or chopped grass, from the silo behind the milking barn. Grant learned to drive a tractor when he was seven. His father would follow along beside the tractor through the fields after spring plowing, picking up stones that had been forced up by the frost and tossing them into the bucket on the tractor. Driving the tractor is still one of the things Grant loves most about farming.

He moves slowly down the yearlings' trough, filling it first with silage and then by hand with grain, while the young cows crowd together to get at the food, trumpeting like elephants with excitement and gratitude.

When Grant finishes here, he will feed and water the twenty-three broiler chickens and seven turkeys he is raising this year for a 4-H project. The chickens lead a short life in a corner of a small barn that one hundred years ago housed horses and carriages for the Nelsons then living on this farm. Eight weeks after Grant starts feeding the chicks, he will have the broilers butchered. He will sell some of the chickens to neighbors in Ryegate Corner. When Thanksgiving comes, he will do the same with the fattened turkeys. As part of his project, he is recording how much it costs to feed and raise these birds and to have them slaughtered. These costs will tell him what the market price should be for the meat when he sells it. It is another lesson in farming.

At nine-fifteen, Jenny leaves for her mail route. When Jenny married Bill she was a schoolteacher who had never lived on a farm. Bill never did ask her to be his wife. He asked her what she thought about farming. She understood that marrying Bill would mean moving to this farm where Bill's family has always lived and learning to love a life of getting up at dawn, eating supper long after dark, freezing in the barnyard in winter, sweating in the milking parlor in summer, and being bound to the cows when everyone else has gone on vacation. Jenny gave up teaching school and learned to milk.

The mail route is a small part of the other work she has learned to do for the farm. Twice a day, and once on Saturday mornings, she drives three miles to the post office in East Ryegate and collects the mail for Ryegate Corner. Then she brings it back to the local post office and waits with her neighbors for it to be sorted. When she signed the contract with the government two years ago to make the short daily delivery, Jenny wondered how she would find time to squeeze one more thing into her family's days, but farms have always forced the families who sustain them to lead lives as elastic as rubber bands. In 1977 the Nelsons bought a tractor and paid for it in three years. Because the United States is now producing more milk than it needs, farmers are receiving less for their milk than they did in 1977, and Jenny says the Nelsons could not afford to buy a new tractor now. The money she earns on the mail route helps the family to stay on the farm.

While Jenny is gone, the cattle dealer and the veterinarian arrive. Hannah dislikes these visits by the cattle dealer, but everyone knows they are necessary. Paul Pearl, the hired man, haggles with the dealer over the price to be paid for the twin bull and heifer calves born this week. A modern dairy farm relies on artificial insemination to breed its cows, so it has no use for bull calves or for their twin sisters, who are usually sterile. All four will be sold for veal. When a fair price has been agreed upon, Paul carries the calves to the dealer's truck and places them with other calves from other farms in the area.

The veterinarian's job on the farm is more complicated, and his visits are less predictable. He may come every day for three weeks to tend to some business and then not be needed again for a month.

The first thing Bill asks him to turn to this morning is a cow that had a hard time calving yesterday. This cow has not been able to push out the sac in which the calf grew for nine months inside her womb. The vet quickly cleans her out. Then he gives a checkup to a cow that had trouble getting pregnant again after the birth of her last calf. Bill wants him to make sure she is ready now to hold her place in the rhythms of the dairy farm. Any cow who does not breed back quickly on a dairy farm will find she is no longer needed. Next he gives a shot to Tyke, the Nelson family kitten.

Finally, the veterinarian goes to look at Andrew's show calf, Premie. Every calf older than six months has to be tested for tuberculosis, and Premie's test shot from three days ago needs to be checked to make sure she is clear of the disease. He checks also to make sure that Premie is healing from her ring-

worm infection. If she were not getting better under Andrew's daily doses of medicine and sunshine, she could not be shown at the 4-H competition tomorrow, and all Andrew's work with her these past few months would be lost. However, the vet says Premie is doing just fine.

By ten-thirty in the morning, everyone is ready for a break. Jenny has finished her mail delivery and spent an hour in the kitchen. The children, who grabbed their breakfasts on their way to their chores several hours earlier, are ready to light briefly at the table and find out how the day will unroll. The last cow has been milked, and Bill's father is cleaning up the milking parlor. Bill has filled the family's milk jar from the bulk tank and is crossing back to the house from the milking parlor. It is more than five hours since this farm came to life, and it is time for the men to eat a real breakfast.

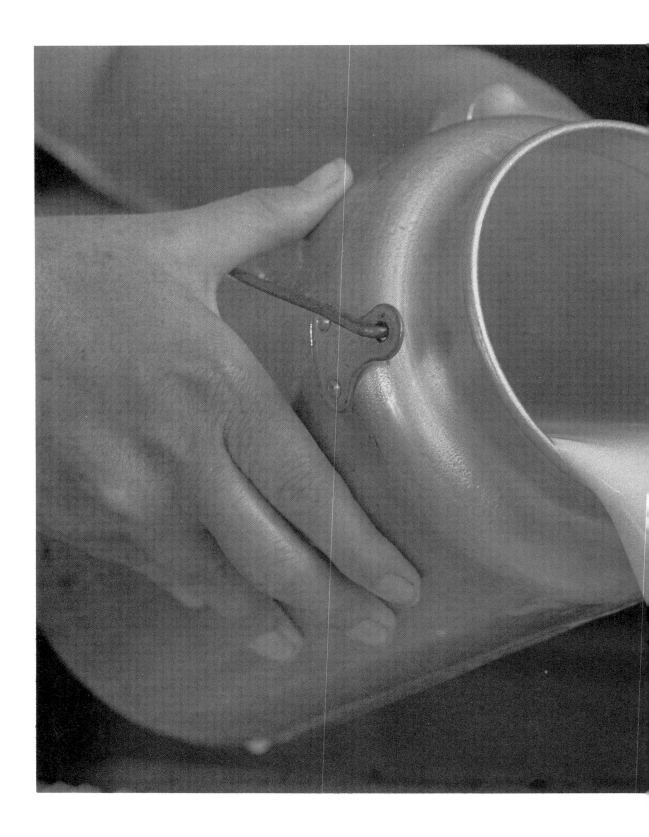

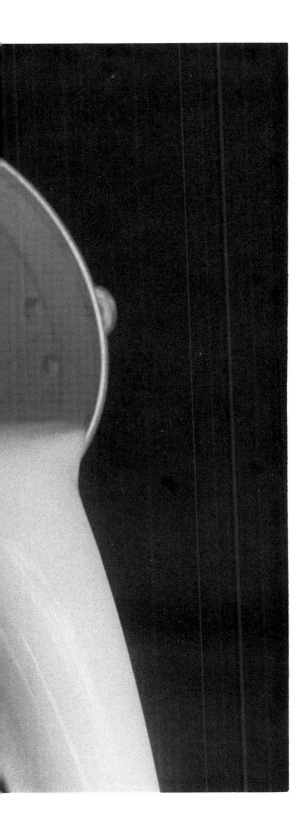

The Nelsons say grace at every meal, even breakfast, giving thanks for the blessings of their life and the strength to live it. In a country where farming was once the major occupation, only one family in sixty now contributes what the Nelsons do to putting food on their table. The milk is just hours old, fresh from the bulk tank. It is rich milk, and it has a rich color, bright white with a halo of pale blue. Small clots of cream float in it like icebergs. Unlike the milk sold in most stores, this milk is not pasteurized. That means it has not been heated quickly to kill any germs and then cooled just as quickly to preserve its sweet taste. Neither has it been homogenized, that is, whirled and shaken violently to break up the fat and make the milk, when it is poured, as smooth as a sheet of white satin. These are jobs for the dairy, which will also bottle the milk and deliver it to stores where it will be bought by customers who have confidence in its high quality. The Nelsons have their own faith in this milk. They drink six quarts of it each day and do not need a dairy to convince them of its goodness.

The maple syrup on the cereal is also from the farm. Last March when sugaring weather arrived, Grant and Andrew went up to the old sugar bush behind their house with their cousins Matt and Ethan, who live on the neighboring farm. Together they tapped fifty maple trees, some of which are the oldest living things on the farm. Every afternoon after school the four boys gathered sap and later boiled it down until they had three gallons of syrup, which they divided between the families. The amber syrup is like liquid candy, thick and sweet, and as pure as the milk that washes it down.

Here at this meal, around this table, the day's work is planned. Until now, everyone has been doing what needs to be done every day at the same time. Late in the afternoon, the day's work will once again fall into a regular pattern. But during the hours in between, each day has a chance to be different.

Bill, Grant, and Paul consider how to share the afternoon's work with Bill's brother, Fremont, who owns the farm next door. Although Bill and Fremont each own a tractor, chuck wagon, and bucketloader, they share two farm trucks, harrowers, plows, a chopper, haying equipment, and other machinery they don't need every day. After Bill talks to Fremont on the telephone, it is decided that Grant, Paul, and Fremont's hired man, Darryl, will begin cut-

ting and chopping the fields that Bill owns eight miles away on the banks of the Connecticut River in Woodsville, New Hampshire. If they finish, they will move on to the fields north of the house.

But first Grant and Andrew must finish their calf records. Both boys are showing calves tomorrow at the 4-H fair in Lyndonville. For Grant, who already has a drawerful of ribbons, it will be his third year of competition. It is Andrew's first.

Andrew chose Premie from all the calves his father offered to him because, quite simply, he loves her. She is a guernsey, a softly colored brown-and-white cow on a farm of black-and-white holsteins. She is small for her age and has had ringworm, but Andrew has not been interested in choosing another calf whose chances of winning a ribbon might be better. He has memorized her pedigree, which is a cow's family tree, and calculated the costs of all the milk, grain, water, and hay she has eaten during the first year of her life. Now he knows what she is worth. Several nights earlier he traveled fifty miles with his mother, brother, and sisters to be tested on this information by a 4-H judge who wanted to know whether he had learned the kinds of lessons he needs to learn to be a good farmer. Now Andrew makes sure that Premie's records are complete so that he can show her in the competition tomorrow.

This year, for the first time, Bill let Grant buy a calf for showing. With his uncle Fremont, Grant went to a cattle club auction last April and came home with a heifer named Lindale-Valley Persuader Madge. He calls her Madge. Madge is a holstein yearling, meaning she is more than a year old but less than two. Grant believes she has the dairiness that he is learning to look for in young stock. He has made all the calculations that Andrew has about feed costs, and like his brother, he has learned the value of his own work as well as the value of his heifer.

Bill helps his sons with the records because he knows the worth of the lessons his sons are learning. Only a part of the work of the farm is done in the fields and barns. An important part is done when Bill sits down every month to look at the new information he has received from the Dairy Herd Improvement Association. Once a month, this association weighs each of the

Nelsons' cows and tests its milk for butterfat and protein content. The association then sends Bill a herd profile telling him how much milk he is getting from each cow and its quality. Bill uses these figures to manage his herd, to decide which cows are no longer able to supply milk in the quantity and quality he needs.

As soon as Andrew finishes his paperwork, he rushes into his bathing suit. He, Hannah, and Betsey are due at swimming lessons at nearby Ticklenaked Pond. Jenny drives them there down a long hill rippling with green corn. They have seen this view so often they hardly notice the cornstalks lapping against the sides of the road like gentle waves. Their thoughts are on the beach.

On a small stretch of sand tucked between the green sea of corn and the darker green water of the pond, nearly fifty children swarm like ants, waiting for the lessons to start. Andrew, Hannah, and Betsey know every child here. They are related to at least ten of them. Their teacher is Nancy Perkins, Bill Nelson's cousin. She is also Andrew's teacher at Blue Mountain Elementary School. There, she is Mrs. Perkins. Here, she is Aunt Nancy. Like his brother and sisters, Andrew makes these adjustments naturally. He has always lived in this town of one hundred people, where the families are as intricately connected as a spider's web.

Grant has outgrown swimming lessons and grown into a man's work on the farm. He is headed with Paul and Darryl to the fields along the Connecticut River that his father bought years ago when the Nelsons needed more land to grow feed for their cows. It costs more to have the land so far from the farm, but it is rich river bottomland, free of stone and good for growing corn.

Haying has the grand and graceful movement of ballet. No words are spoken. Grant drives the tractor in a sweeping circle around the field, turning his head back and forth between the open, uncut grass ahead and the line of hay lying cut behind him. Fifty yards behind, Paul drives another tractor that gathers the cut hay into a long pile and blows it in a stream into the truck that Darryl is driving behind him. The air grows heavy and sweet. As the circle shrinks with each pass of the machinery, Grant gradually gains on Darryl's

truck until he has moved from the head of the line to its tail. Most of the hay lands in the truck, but gradually the air fills with dust, a harvest of hay confetti that showers down on everyone. Three passes around the field fill the truck. Then the men must make the round trip to Ryegate to dump the haylage in a bunker silo behind the milking barn, where Bill will pack it down later with the bucketloader. The work is hot and tiring, but Grant likes it.

When Andrew, Betsey, and Hannah finish swimming lessons, they have their own fields to work. Two years ago the Nelsons planted two hundred raspberry bushes behind their house. The long hot days of summer have ripened the fruit and filled the bushes with plump berries. Jenny has given Hannah and Betsey responsibility for harvesting this crop. Hannah moves down the rows with wooden baskets, filling quart after quart with raspberries as small and perfect as her thumbnail and red as rubies. The Nelsons use the

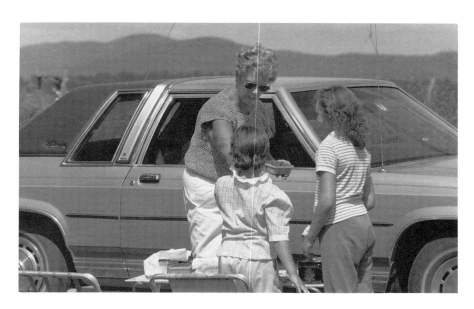

berries freely, sprinkling them on cereal, burying them in muffins, and heaping them in pies. Hannah takes the pints and quarts they don't need and puts them up for sale on a table by the road. It is more money for the farm and some for Hannah's and Betsey's pockets.

Andrew and Betsey aren't raising enough in their gardens this summer to sell any of their produce, but their harvests will be picked, eaten, canned, frozen, or dried for their family. Both have 4-H gardens. The 4-H has supplied them with seeds, and they have been responsible for preparing garden beds, planting their seeds, and tending their plots. Andrew is raising lettuce, carrots, cucumbers, onions, and beans. Betsey grew vegetables last year. This year she is trying marigolds, bachelor buttons, zinnias, nasturtiums, and asters.

Jenny works beside them on her tomatoes and broccoli, while Betsey picks grass that is creeping up around her flowers. Andrew thins his vegetable beds, pulling up sweet young carrots no bigger than his fingers and absentmindedly eating them down to the fringed heads. When he discovers that his cucumber

leaves are being eaten by bugs, he calls to his father, who is in front of the barn tinkering with a broken truck. Bill puts down his tools and comes over. He takes his children's work as seriously as his own because he knows their work is as necessary as his if this farm is to survive. Now he bends his head low over the cucumber leaves with Andrew and offers advice. Farming has always been a war of sorts, and Bill wants his children to learn how to use a farmer's weapons. Together they agree that some vegetable dust may kill the uninvited guests.

Twice a summer, a 4-H inspector comes to visit every garden project. When she arrives today, she checks for such things as loose soil, straight rows, insect control, good growth for the season, and mulching. It is tough work to be graded on because a gardener can do everything well, as Andrew does, and still lose a crop, as Andrew lost his pumpkins earlier this year. But both Andrew and Betsey score high today. It is a good sign. The county fair is only a month away, and a good score here puts them in the running for a red or blue ribbon there, and perhaps a cash prize, too.

As Jenny goes into the kitchen, she takes Andrew's lettuce thinnings with her. It is two o'clock, time for the Nelsons' midday dinner. Nothing that can be eaten is wasted.

Dinner on the farm is a big meal, the only one where everyone sits down together. It is full of chatter and interruptions, which everyone accepts as a fact of life on the farm. First the UPS truck comes to deliver three boxes of machinery parts. Bill and Paul get up to open the boxes and make sure that the parts needed to fix the chuck wagon have arrived. For the past few days Bill has had to borrow his brother Fremont's chuck wagon twice a day to feed the cows. A few minutes later, Bill, Grant, and Paul go out to greet the salesman from the Independent Buyers Association. This is a general farm store on wheels. The big red van goes from farm to farm and saves farmers the trouble of running into town on small errands for the thousands of things they need. Grant wants a special shampoo for Madge for the show tomorrow, Bill buys a balling gun for giving pills to cows, penicillin for an ailing cow, jugs of cleanser and acid for the milking-machine pipeline, and a pair of boots for Paul. No sooner does everyone rejoin the dinner table than the grain truck arrives. The grain truck will take two and a half hours to unload its 44,000 pounds of grain into the barns around the farm. It is the most expensive visit anyone makes to the farm, and the grain will be gone in a month.

Visits like this throughout the day make the Nelson farm seem like a small sun in the center of a large solar system. In rural parts of the country like Vermont, where farming is a way of life for many families, much of the business in the area revolves around the business of the farm. Jenny often speaks to groups around Vermont about the important part that farms play in the country's business. To make her point, she climbs on a chair and unrolls a

list of fifty names of businesses the Nelson farm helps support. The list includes the names of the plumber who fixes the watering system in the barns, the electrical supply store where the Nelsons get the large bulbs for the milking parlor, a sawmill where Bill buys sawdust for bedding, a gas station where he fills up his trucks, three insurance companies, a lawyer, and a bank. It is clear that if this farm were to fail, its collapse would be felt far beyond the borders of these fields.

When the meal is over, the last of the Nelsons scatter from the dinner table. Jenny, Hannah, and Betsey shuttle between the dining room and the kitchen, clearing and washing the dishes, but as soon as the housework is done, the farmwork begins again. Betsey crosses the road to the milking parlor where Andrew and his friend Josh have tied up Premie in the bright afternoon sun for a bath.

Grant and Andrew are both learning the hard way that there are advantages to choosing a show calf with naturally dark markings in those places like the backs of the back legs where cows tend to get dirty. Before Madge is clean, Grant will have scrubbed her from head to hoof and bleached her flanks with diluted Clorox to bring out the black-and-white markings of a prize holstein.

Andrew doesn't face quite as many problems because Premie's soft brown color covers her where he needs it most, but he leads Josh and Betsey through a thorough cleaning and brushing until Premie shines like a new penny. Then Jenny helps Andrew clean Premie's ears with baby oil and swabs. Premie may never again look as good as she will for the next twenty-four hours, but that is all Andrew cares about. Tomorrow the judges will look in her ears, consider the trim of her hoofs, lift her tail, and run their hands over her haircut. Andrew wants them to find no fault.

Bill is never far from all this activity. In the summer, when Bill leaves the farm to plow or hay eight miles away in Woodsville, Andrew misses him. He is used to having his father close at hand. When Betsey begins to miss her best friend from school, who lives so far away that they have to write letters to each other during the summer, she goes out to be with her father in the milking parlor. Bill is as constant as the weather in the life of this farm and in the lives of his children.

Even now he is casually keeping an eye on Andrew's and Grant's work with their calves although he is haying a field one hundred yards up the road with Paul. The field lies just below the Ryegate Corner cemetery, where Nelsons have been buried for two hundred years. So many of them lie there that it is difficult to find a view of the farm from the cemetery that does not include a Nelson headstone. These are Bill's ancestors and the ancestors of his children.

Each time the truck is full of haylage, Bill makes a full circle from the fields below the cemetery to his children bathing their calves outside the milking parlor, looping around them like a needle pulling thread that ties everyone together.

By late afternoon it is time to start milking again. Bill, his father, and Paul head into the milking parlor. They must rinse all the milking equipment again and ready the stalls for the cows. Jenny, who likes this part of the day more

than any other, crosses from the house to the edge of the pasture and ducks under the electric fence. The children follow her, and everyone scatters into the pasture to drive the cows to the barn.

For more than half an hour the fields are noisy with the songs of cows lowing and Jenny and the children calling, "Heeey, uh. Come on, girl." The cows are dull and lazy in the afternoon heat. Andrew and Betsey take the near pasture, using canes and sticks to prod the cows to their feet and point them toward the barn. The cows lumber along, their udders swinging heavily beneath them, as if they had all the time in the world. Hannah and Jenny head for the far edge of the pasture, a quarter of a mile away. They clamber over stone walls that have been built by Nelsons and the settlers before them over two hundred years of stone-picking. They will bring home the cows that have

melted into the cool shade of the trees. They need to be careful because it is easy to lose a black-and-white cow in the shadows and because during calving time, every cow has to be accounted for at every milking. If a cow has calved, Bill needs to know.

From a ridge near the edge of this far pasture, with her uncle Fremont's farm at her back, Hannah looks across a green valley to the farm where her great-grandfather still lives. That farm has been in the Nelson family for more than two centuries. It is the farm where her grandfather and his brother grew up and where they learned to farm. Forty-four years ago, when it became clear that that farm could not support Harold Nelson, his brother, and their

father, Hannah's great-grandfather helped her grandfather buy the family's farm from a cousin whose children did not want to go into farming. Her great-grandfather's farm is now owned by one of Bill's cousins.

More than her sister and her brothers, Hannah can understand those distant cousins who chose not to farm. Although she carries her full share of the children's farm chores, Hannah is not sure she wants to stay on a farm all her life. She is not sure that she wants to work this way or this hard or take a vacation only every three years.

It will be her choice. Bill and Jenny want their children to make up their own minds about farming after they have finished college. That is the same choice Bill's father gave him and the same choice Jenny had when she married

Bill. But it is plain that Bill and Jenny hope this farm will stay in the Nelson family, and it is also plain that Grant expects to spend his life on this farm. He likes the idea that his cousin Ethan will probably own his uncle's farm next door, and that he and his closest friend will probably be able to get up every morning of their lives and look across to the other's farm. If their other children decide to farm, Bill and Jenny want to help them buy a farm nearby, keeping them close to the fields and families where they have their roots.

Right now this farm is enough for everyone. Out in the pasture, Betsey and Hannah are hunting for twin calves born early this morning. The calves are hiding, quiet and still, in sheltered pockets of warmth among the long tufts of grass. They are waiting for their mother, who will be spared the evening milking in order to feed them, to come and claim them. When Betsey and Hannah find the calves and make sure they are fine, the two girls duck back under the electric fence and cross the road to the heifer barn to do their evening chores of feeding and watering.

Grant and Andrew are already in the barnyard, practicing again leading their calves for the show tomorrow. Madge likes these walks. She goes wherever Grant leads her, stops when he stops, and stands in the position the judges will look for tomorrow. Premie is less cooperative. Andrew pulls and coaxes, pushes and sometimes shouts, but he does not quit. It is his last chance. Tomorrow the judges will be watching carefully how each handler works with his calf. Among the farmer's lessons Andrew has learned from raising Premie this year is that each cow has her own personality. Premie is just plain stubborn.

Finally, at a time when most families are getting up from dinner, Jenny and the children head back to Ticklenaked Pond to wash away the dust and sweat of the day. There are about twenty children splashing in the water in the softening light of evening. None of them is older than fourteen. In this rural area, boys over fifteen are home in the milking parlor. It is unthinkable and impossible for Bill to enjoy such a break in the hot, dry day. Up the hill, where he, his father, and Paul are collecting a small portion of the 1,750,000 pounds of milk the Nelson farm will produce this year, there are still fifty cows waiting to be milked.

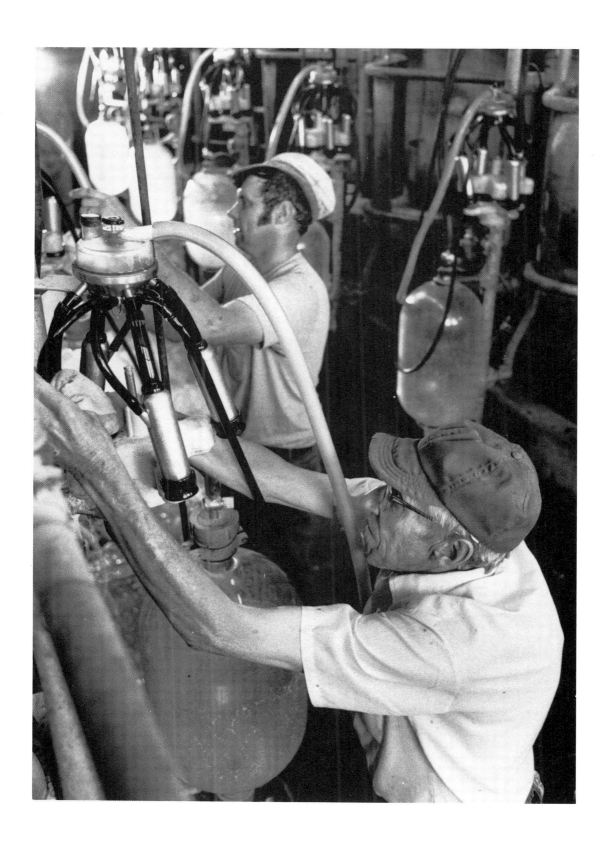

Supper takes barely as long as a breath in the long day. Grant and Andrew hardly pause to take it. It is eight o'clock, and shadows are growing long on the shoulders of the hills, but there is still much to do to get ready for the show tomorrow. Grant polishes his boots until he can see his face in them and tries on a pair of white pants his father wore when he was about his age. Then Grant goes out to the barnyard where Andrew is waiting with Premie for Bill to come and help him with a final trimming. Grant brings Madge out to wait, too.

Bill leaves his father in the milking parlor and comes across the road to the heifer barn where Grant and Andrew are waiting. For a change, Premie is the cooperative one. She calmly eats the daylilies that grow wildly around the barn while Bill and Andrew quickly clip her. But Madge wants no part of this. It takes all Grant's strength to hold his calf while Bill shows him how to use the electric razor to trim Madge's shoulders, back, face, and tail. When Grant tries the razor, Bill takes a turn wrestling Madge. Half a dozen times Grant is ready to give up, but Bill quietly coaxes him along until the job is done.

Tomorrow morning, Bill tells his sons, both calves will need only a spot washing and a good brushing to be ready for the ring. He shows them how to brush the ends of their calves' tails backward to make them full and soft.

Like nearly everything else he is teaching his children about dairy showmanship, Bill learned these lessons from his father thirty years ago on this farm when he started showing calves. In passing these tips along to his sons, Bill is making sure that the arts of dairy farming as they have been practiced by the Nelson family will remain a part of this farm for as long into the future as anyone here can foresee.

By the time the calves are clipped and led back to their freshly made beds of hay in the barn, it is nine-thirty. Daylight is gone. Madge and Premie are as ready as they ever will be, and so are Grant and Andrew — for this show. The boys head to bed. Bill goes back to the milking parlor to help his father finish milking.

The noise of the milking parlor is the last sound to stop on the farm at the end of the day. First the throbbing of the milking machines stops as the last cow is let out of the parlor into the pale blue light of the barn. Then the radio is turned off. Even after the lights have been turned off and Bill and his father have headed to their houses for supper, the milking machinery pumps on

alone, flushing the tubes and pipes one final time. Finally, that, too, stops. Up the road, the church bell that has been calling Nelsons to worship for more than a hundred years peals ten times. When the last echoes of the bells fade, the silence that settles over everything is as deep and dark as the sky.

Bill and Jenny eat their supper at ten-thirty, quietly and alone. Afterward, while Jenny hems Andrew's white pants for the show tomorrow, she and Bill talk about how to get all the chores done in the morning before Fremont comes by at seven with the truck to pick up Grant and Andrew, Madge and Premie. Bill's father and Paul, the hired man, will finish the morning milking so Bill, Jenny, Hannah, and Betsey can leave for the fair by eight-thirty. Jenny will pack a picnic. A substitute will make her mail runs tomorrow. No swimming lessons will be held tomorrow because nearly all the children in Ryegate will be going to the fair. It will be a rare summer holiday for everyone.

The last thing Bill and Jenny do before they go to bed is listen to the weather report for tomorrow. The day promises to be the hottest of the entire summer. The sun will rise at 5:23 and set at 8:24. It will be another good day for growing.